SPIDERS

BY GAIL GIBBONS
New and Updated

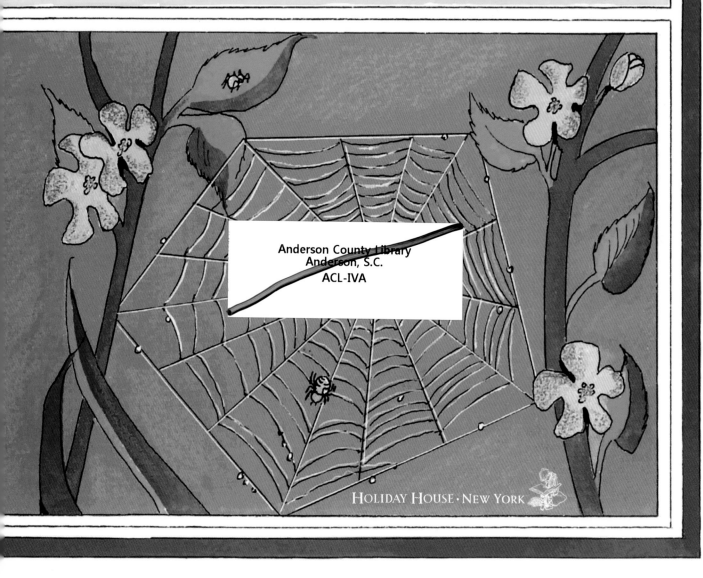

HOLIDAY HOUSE · NEW YORK

To Fred Lyon

Special thanks to Louis N. Sorkin, BCE,
Entomologist, American Museum of
Natural History

Special thanks also to Dr. Gordon Nielsen,
Entomologist, Hinesburg, Vermont

HOLIDAY HOUSE is registered in the
U.S. Patent and Trademark Office.
Printed and bound in July 2020 at Tien Wah Press,
Johor Bahru, Johor, Malaysia.
www.holidayhouse.com
Second Edition
1 3 5 7 9 10 8 6 4 2

Library of Congress has cataloged the prior edition as follows:

Library of Congress Cataloging-in-Publication Data

Gibbons, Gail.
Spiders / written and illustrated by Gail Gibbons.
    p. cm.
    Summary: Examines the physical characteristics,
    behavior, habitats and different kinds of spiders
    ISBN 0-8234-1006-4
    1. Spiders—Juvenile literature. [1. Spiders.] I. Title
    QL458.4.G53   1993   92-54414   CIP   AC
    595.4'4—dc20

    ISBN 978-0-8234-4723-7 (hardcover)
    ISBN 978-0-8234-1081-1 (trade paper)

Spiders may look scary but most of them don't hurt people. There are almost fifty thousand different kinds of spiders.

Spiders come in many shapes and sizes. Some are so tiny that they are no bigger than a speck of dust.

Others can be as big as a dinner plate. Most spiders are brown, gray, or black. Some have bright colors.

The first spiders lived about 400 million years ago, even before dinosaurs roamed the earth.

ARACHNID
(uh•RACK•nid)

Spiders belong to a group of animals called arachnids.
The word *arachnid* comes from an old Greek legend.
Once there was a woman named Arachne who was angry
when she lost a weaving contest against the Goddess
Athena. When Arachne died, Athena turned Arachne's
body into a spider so she could weave forever.

A Spider's Body

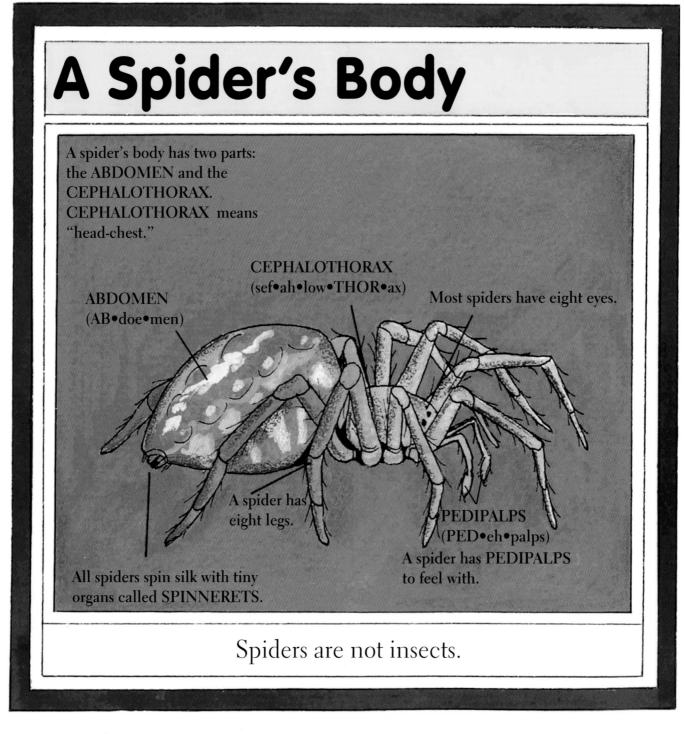

A spider's body has two parts: the ABDOMEN and the CEPHALOTHORAX. CEPHALOTHORAX means "head-chest."

CEPHALOTHORAX
(sef•ah•low•THOR•ax)

Most spiders have eight eyes.

ABDOMEN
(AB•doe•men)

A spider has eight legs.

PEDIPALPS
(PED•eh•palps)

A spider has PEDIPALPS to feel with.

All spiders spin silk with tiny organs called SPINNERETS.

Spiders are not insects.

An Insect's Body

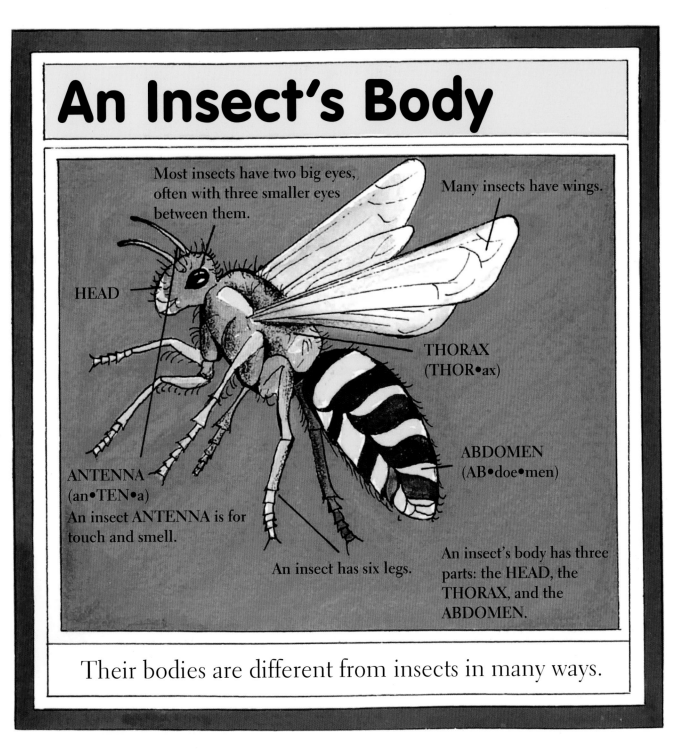

Most insects have two big eyes, often with three smaller eyes between them.

Many insects have wings.

HEAD

THORAX
(THOR•ax)

ANTENNA
(an•TEN•a)
An insect ANTENNA is for touch and smell.

ABDOMEN
(AB•doe•men)

An insect has six legs.

An insect's body has three parts: the HEAD, the THORAX, and the ABDOMEN.

Their bodies are different from insects in many ways.

Most male spiders are smaller than female spiders. When a male spider finds a mate, he must be careful. If the female spider is hungry, she might eat him. Some male spiders do a dance and bring an insect to attract a female.

Most mother spiders lay their eggs and enclose them in a strong, silk egg sac. Some spiders lay a few eggs. Others lay thousands. After a number of weeks, the baby spiders creep out of the silk sac. Spider babies are called spiderlings.

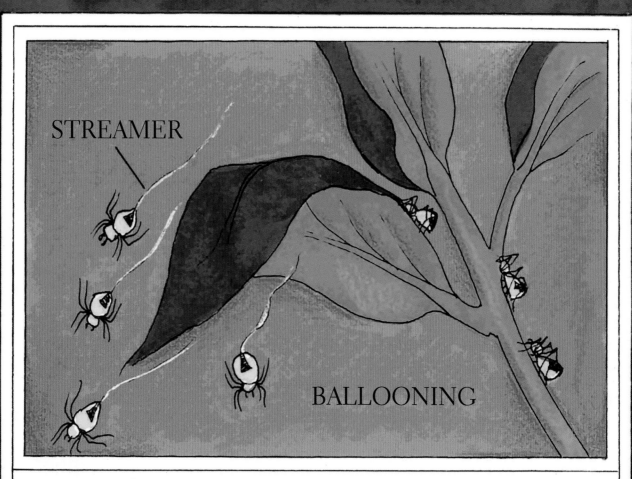

STREAMER

BALLOONING

Most spider mothers don't stay with their babies. Some spiderlings care for themselves as soon as they are born. They run up to the highest places they can find. The spiderlings then spin out long streamers of silk. A breeze lifts them and carries them to their new homes. This way of travel is called ballooning.

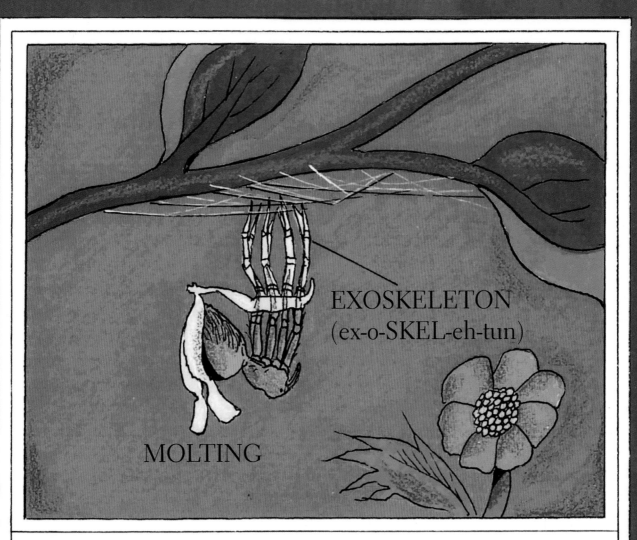

EXOSKELETON
(ex-o-SKEL-eh-tun)

MOLTING

As a spiderling grows, its hard outer skin, called an exoskeleton, becomes tight. The skin tears near the legs and along the abdominal sides. The spider sheds this skin by climbing out. This is called molting. Most spiders molt five to ten times.

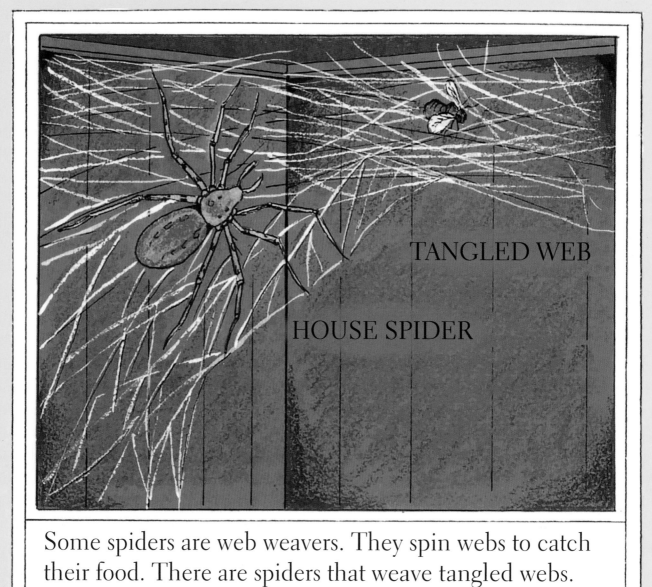

TANGLED WEB

HOUSE SPIDER

Some spiders are web weavers. They spin webs to catch their food. There are spiders that weave tangled webs. The spider spins a tangled mass of silk. When an insect is trapped, the spider runs out to get it.

SHEET WEB

LINYPHIID SPIDER

Other spiders weave sheet webs. The spider hangs upside down beneath the web. When an insect hits the sheet web, the spider quickly pulls it through the webbing.

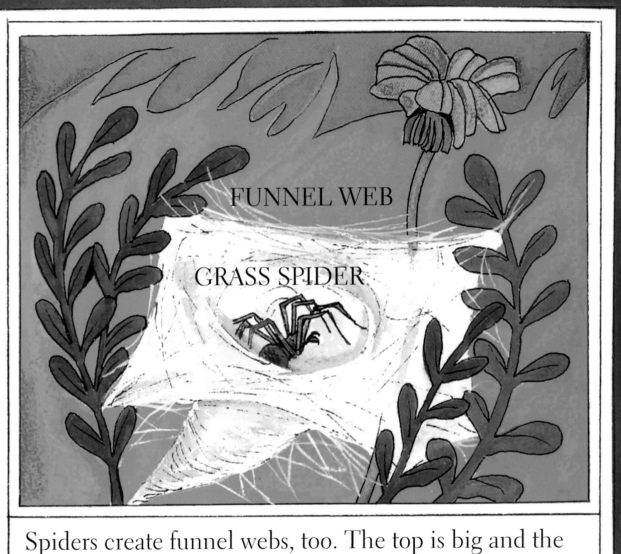

FUNNEL WEB

GRASS SPIDER

Spiders create funnel webs, too. The top is big and the bottom is small. The web is held in place by lines of silk. The spider sits in the funnel, and waits for an insect to fly or walk in.

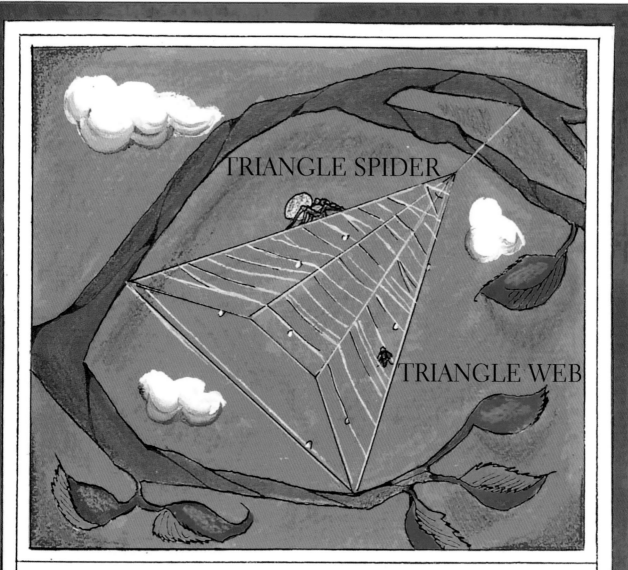

TRIANGLE SPIDER

TRIANGLE WEB

Some spiders spin triangle webs. A triangle web is
fastened at three points. The web's bands of dry and
sticky silk trap insects.

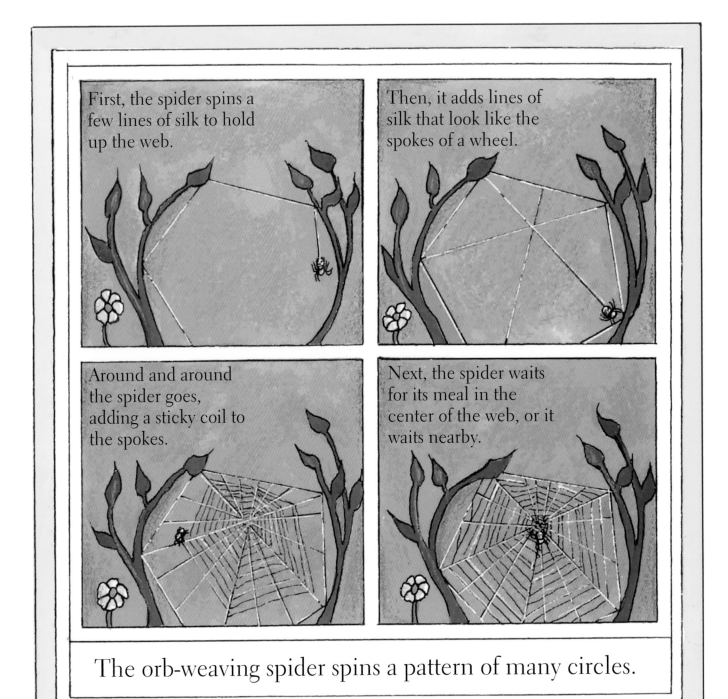

First, the spider spins a few lines of silk to hold up the web.

Then, it adds lines of silk that look like the spokes of a wheel.

Around and around the spider goes, adding a sticky coil to the spokes.

Next, the spider waits for its meal in the center of the web, or it waits nearby.

The orb-weaving spider spins a pattern of many circles.

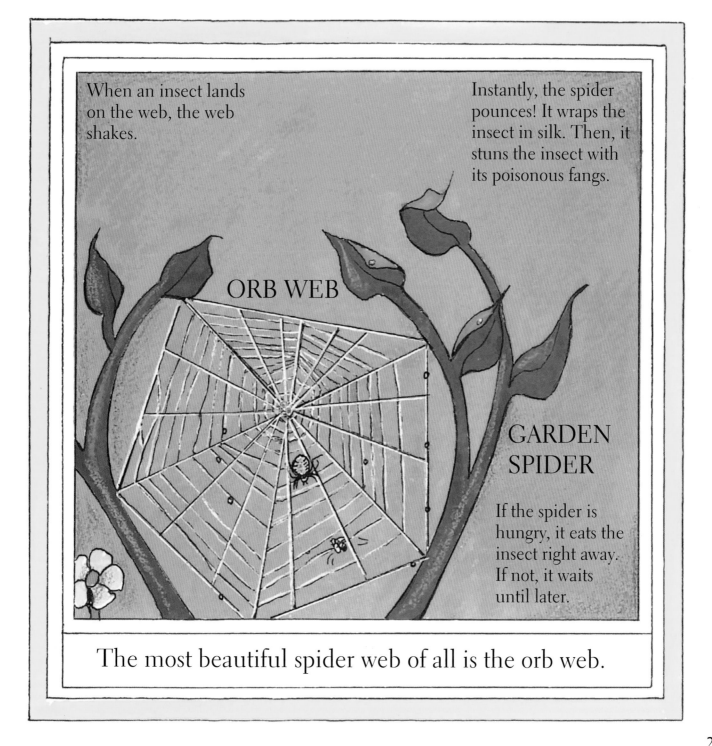

When an insect lands on the web, the web shakes.

Instantly, the spider pounces! It wraps the insect in silk. Then, it stuns the insect with its poisonous fangs.

ORB WEB

GARDEN SPIDER

If the spider is hungry, it eats the insect right away. If not, it waits until later.

The most beautiful spider web of all is the orb web.

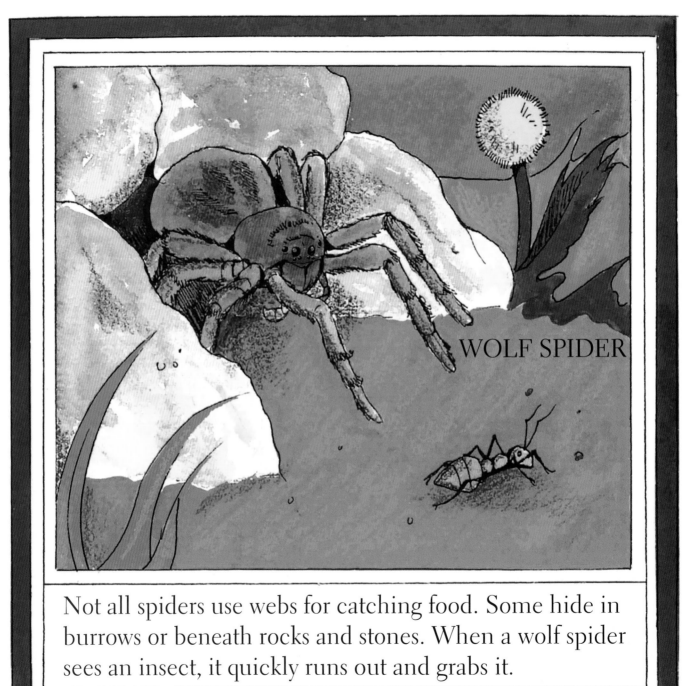

WOLF SPIDER

Not all spiders use webs for catching food. Some hide in burrows or beneath rocks and stones. When a wolf spider sees an insect, it quickly runs out and grabs it.

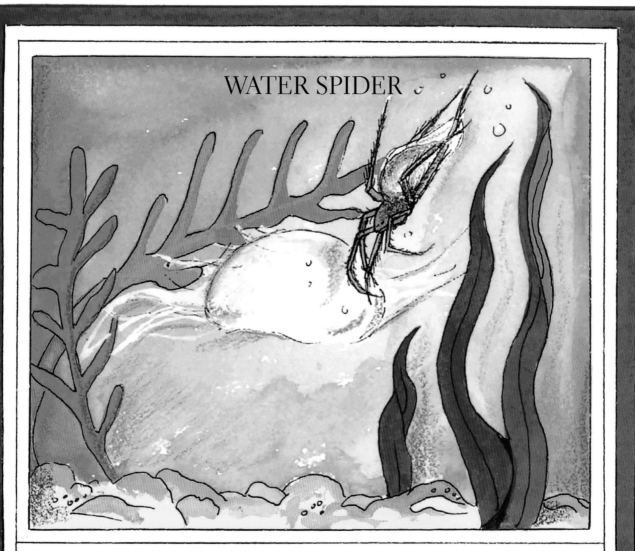

WATER SPIDER

One unusual kind of spider lives underwater. It weaves a bell-shaped web. Then it fills the web with tiny air bubbles stuck on its body hairs. The spider stays there, breathing the air from the bubbles, and waits to catch water insects.

TRAPDOOR SPIDER

Another type of spider digs a tunnel and lines it with silk. To protect itself, it makes a hinged trapdoor from dirt and silk to cover the tunnel. When the spider is hungry, it opens the door a bit. If an insect comes close, the spider scurries out to catch it.

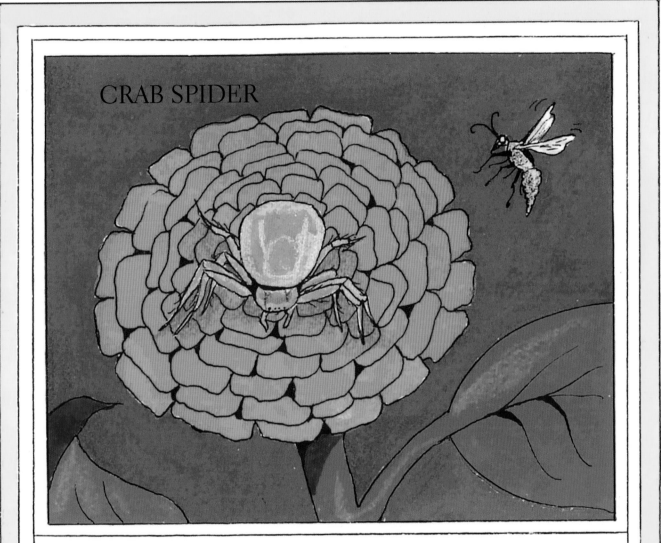

CRAB SPIDER

Some spiders hide on or inside flowers. One spider even changes color, from yellow to white, to match the color of the flower. When an insect lands, the spider snatches it.

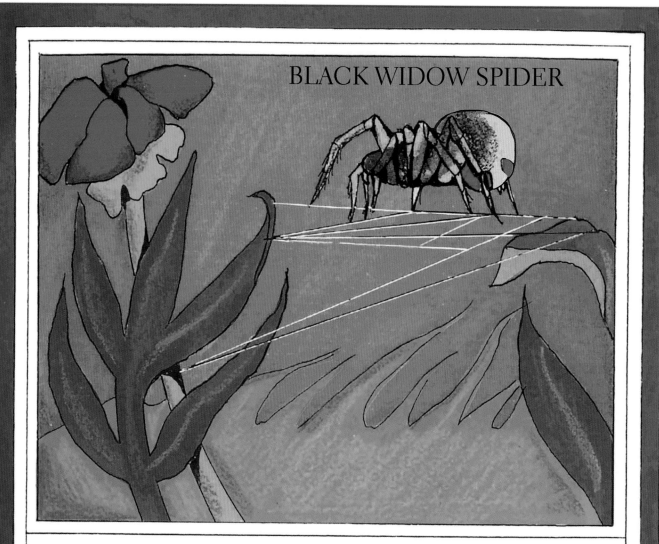

BLACK WIDOW SPIDER

Some spiders are dangerous. One of them is the black widow spider. The black widow spider bites only when its web is disturbed or it is in danger. The venom of a black widow spider can kill a person.

TARANTULA

The biggest spiders of all are the tarantulas. When its legs are stretched out, it can measure about ten inches wide. It is very hairy. Tarantulas that live in the United States are not poisonous to people.

Spiders have enemies. Some insects, like spider wasps, hunt and eat spiders. Toads, frogs, and some birds like to eat spiders, too.

Most spiders live for about one year, but some live two to three years. Female tarantulas can live to be 25 years old.

Many people don't like spiders because they are afraid of them. But spiders help us. They play an important role by eating many insects that are harmful to crops and people.

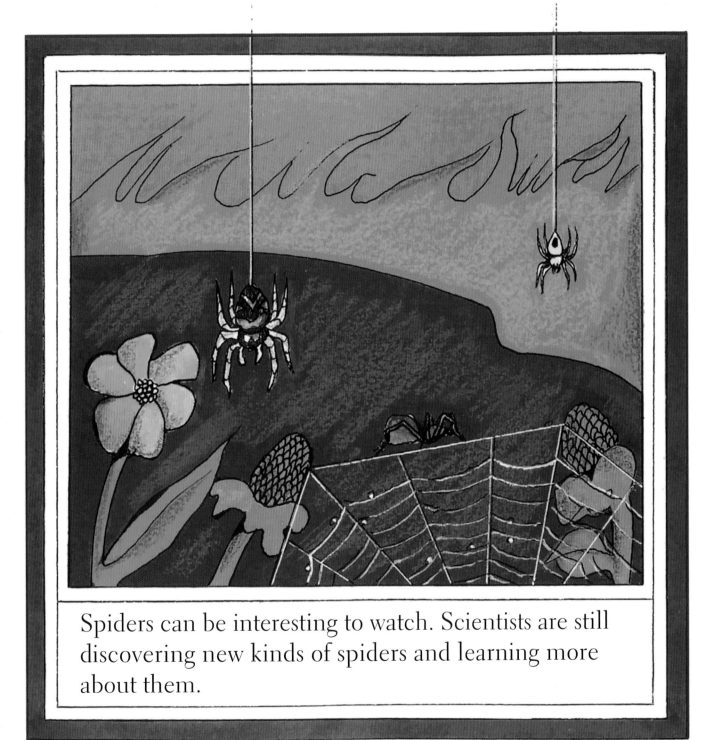

Spiders can be interesting to watch. Scientists are still discovering new kinds of spiders and learning more about them.

Spiders... spiders... spiders!

 Remember the nursery rhyme "Little Miss Muffet"? Little Miss Muffet was a real little girl. Her father was a spider expert who used to make her eat mashed spiders when she was sick. About 200 years ago, this was a common cold remedy.

A person who is terrified of spiders has arachnophobia (uh•rack•ni•FOE•bee•uh).

 Spider silk is three times stronger than steel thread the same thickness.

Some spiders spin a special line called a dragline. If an enemy comes, the spider can quickly drop down the dragline and escape.

 Some spiders can walk on water. The raft spider does this by spreading its legs wide while it takes quick steps.

 The deadliest spider in the world is the Brazilian wandering spider.

Not many animals eat ants because they taste bad. Some spiders are protected because they look like an ant. They are called ant mimics.

 Spiders have an excellent sense of touch. Their bodies, mouths, and legs are covered with fine sensory hairs.

 Spiders don't stick to their own webs because their feet are specially shaped.

 Spiders can walk up walls and across ceilings, because they have special grip pads on their feet.

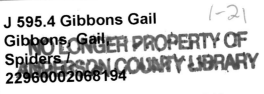